Solar Energy Innovations: Beyond Solar Panels

Contents

Preface

Introduction

Chapter 1: Introduction to Solar Energy

Chapter 2: Concentrated Solar Power (CSP) Technology

Chapter 3: Solar Water Heating and Thermal Energy

Chapter 4: Solar Windows and Building-Integrated Photovoltaics (BIPV)

Chapter 5: Solar Paint and Coatings

Chapter 6: Solar Energy in Space

Chapter 7: Solar-Powered Transportation

Chapter 8: Agrivoltaics: Solar Energy and Agriculture

Chapter 9: Solar Energy Storage Innovations

Chapter 10: The Future of Solar Energy: What's Next?

Glossary

Preface

The maritime and offshore industries are facing transformative times, with rapid advancements in technology, stricter regulatory frameworks, and an ever-growing need for enhanced operational safety and compliance. Recognizing the need for practical, accessible, and targeted knowledge, the Gosships Learning Series was created to offer industry professionals the tools they need to stay ahead of these changes.

This series is designed to provide foundational to intermediate knowledge, with a focus on practical application and real-world relevance. Each book in the series is coupled with a certification test, ensuring that the knowledge gained is not only understood but can also be effectively applied in professional settings.

The Gosships Learning Series is meant to empower maritime and energy sector personnel, from entry-level crew members to shoreside managers, by equipping them with the skills needed to navigate the complexities of modern operations. We hope this series will support your professional development and open new opportunities for growth and success in your career.

Introduction

Welcome to the *Gosships Learning Series*, a comprehensive collection designed for professionals seeking to expand their knowledge and advance their careers in the maritime and energy sectors. This book, *Solar Energy Innovations: Beyond Solar Panels*, explores the transformative power of solar energy and its applications beyond the traditional photovoltaic (PV) panels. Crafted by experienced regulators and industry executives, this resource ensures that the information provided is both authoritative and aligned with current industry standards. Whether you're new to the subject or looking to deepen your expertise, this book will give you the insights you need to stay ahead in the ever-evolving field of solar energy.

In this book, we will explore the following key areas:

- **Emerging Solar Technologies**: Discover advancements beyond conventional solar panels, such as solar thermal systems, solar concentrators, and building-integrated photovoltaics (BIPV).

- **Energy Storage for Solar Power**: Learn about the latest innovations in energy storage systems that complement solar energy generation, making it more reliable and efficient.

- **Integration with Smart Grids**: Understand how solar power is being integrated into modern energy grids, enabling better energy distribution and efficiency.

- **Solar Energy for Industrial Applications**: Explore how solar energy is transforming industries beyond residential use, from agriculture to large-scale industrial operations.

- **Environmental and Economic Considerations**: Examine the economic viability and environmental benefits of solar energy, including its role in reducing greenhouse gas emissions and promoting sustainability.

- **Global Trends in Solar Energy**: Dive into the latest trends and policies driving solar energy adoption worldwide, and how these innovations are shaping the future of clean energy.

After reading this book, you will be prepared to take an assessment that tests your understanding of the material. Upon successful completion, you can obtain a *Certificate of Achievement* by visiting www.gosships.com and accessing the training platform. This certification will validate your expertise in solar energy innovations and enhance your professional credibility.

Who is this book for?

This book is designed for:

- **Energy sector professionals** seeking to expand their understanding of solar energy innovations.
- **Engineers and technicians** working on the development and implementation of advanced solar technologies.
- **Sustainability officers and decision-makers** responsible for integrating renewable energy solutions within organizations.
- **Students and researchers** interested in the technical and practical applications of solar energy.
- **Government and regulatory personnel** involved in policy-making and implementation of clean energy initiatives.

By mastering the concepts in this book, you'll be equipped to navigate the growing opportunities in solar energy, stay compliant with evolving regulations, and contribute to a more sustainable and energy-efficient future.

Thank you for choosing the *Gosships Learning Series* to support your journey of continuous learning and professional growth.

Gosships Learning Series 2024/2025:

1. Hydrogen: The Fuel of the Future
2. Green Ammonia: The Next Big Thing in Shipping
3. Decarbonizing Shipping: Pathways to Zero Emissions
4. Battery Technology for Industrial Applications
5. Carbon Capture and Storage: Can It Save the Planet?
6. Biofuels 101: Turning Waste into Energy
7. Understanding LNG (Liquefied Natural Gas)
8. Methanol as a Marine Fuel
9. Offshore Wind Energy: The Future of Renewable Power
10. Tidal and Wave Energy: Harnessing the Ocean
11. Electrofuels: The Next Generation of Carbon-Neutral Fuels
12. Energy Storage Systems for Grid Reliability
13. Hydrogen Fuel Cells for Transportation
14. Solar Energy Innovations: Beyond Solar Panels
15. Smart Grids: The Backbone of Future Energy Systems
16. Ammonia-Hydrogen Blends: A Dual Fuel Solution?
17. Nuclear Power: Small Modular Reactors for a Low-Carbon Future
18. Hydropower: The Oldest Renewable Energy Source
19. Decentralized Energy Systems: Microgrids for Resilience
20. Energy Efficiency Technologies for Industry
21. Hydrogen Production from Seawater
22. Fuel Cells for Maritime Applications
23. Geothermal Energy: Unlocking Earth's Heat
24. Future of EV Charging Infrastructure

25. Synthetic Fuels: Bridging the Gap to Decarbonization
26. Cybersecurity for Maritime and Offshore Operations
27. AI and Automation in Shipping and Logistics
28. Digital Twins in Maritime: Revolutionizing Asset Management
29. Risk Management in Offshore and Maritime Operations
30. Compliance with IMO 2020 Regulations
31. Sustainable Ship Design: Reducing Environmental Impact
32. Marine Renewable Energy: Wave, Tidal, and Offshore Wind Integration
33. Ballast Water Management Systems
34. Blockchain Technology in Shipping: Improving Transparency & Efficiency
35. Effective Supply Chain Management for Energy Industries
36. Leadership in the Energy Transition
37. Effective Crisis Management in Maritime Operations
38. Shipyard Safety Management Systems
39. Port State Control (PSC) Inspection Readiness
40. Remote Vessel Operations and Autonomous Shipping
41. Optimizing Fleet Performance with Data Analytics
42. Maritime Environmental Regulations: Staying Ahead of Compliance
43. Advanced Maintenance Strategies: Condition Monitoring & Predictive Maintenance
44. Global LNG Market: Trends and Opportunities
45. Incident Investigation in Maritime Operations
46. International Maritime Law: Key Concepts and Applications
47. Emergency Preparedness and Response for Offshore Oil & Gas
48. Energy Transition Strategies for Oil and Gas Companies

49. Maritime Drones: Applications and Safety Considerations

50. Effective Project Management in Offshore Energy Projects

All Rights Reserved Disclaimer

The content in this book, including text, graphics, images, logos, and designs, is the intellectual property of *Gosships LLC* and is protected under copyright law. No part of this publication may be reproduced, distributed, transmitted, or displayed without the prior written permission of the publisher, except for brief quotations in critical reviews or academic articles.

The information provided in this book is for educational purposes only, supplied "as is," without any warranties. The authors and publishers disclaim liability for any direct or indirect loss or damage arising from the use of material in this book.

For permissions or inquiries, please contact: admin@gosships.com.

© 2024 *Gosships LLC*. All rights reserved.

Chapter 1
Introduction to Solar Energy

Solar energy is a renewable and limitless resource derived from the sun. For centuries, humans have harnessed the sun's energy for warmth and light, but only in recent decades have we developed technologies to convert solar energy into electricity efficiently. The most widely known method of generating solar power is through **Photovoltaic (PV) panels**, which convert sunlight directly into electricity. However, recent innovations have introduced new and exciting ways to capture, store, and use solar energy more effectively.

As the world seeks to reduce its reliance on fossil fuels and transition to cleaner energy sources, solar energy is playing an increasingly critical role. Innovations in solar energy have expanded its application far beyond rooftop panels. From **Concentrated Solar Power (CSP)** to **solar paint**, we are moving into a future where solar energy can be integrated into almost every aspect of modern life. These new technologies not only expand the potential uses of solar power but also address some of the limitations of traditional solar panels, such as efficiency, storage, and scalability.

Chapter 2

Concentrated Solar Power (CSP) Technology

Concentrated Solar Power (CSP) systems are one of the most promising innovations in solar energy. Unlike photovoltaic panels that convert sunlight directly into electricity, CSP systems use mirrors or lenses to focus sunlight onto a small area, typically to heat a fluid. This heat is then used to produce steam that drives a turbine, generating electricity in a similar manner to conventional power plants.

There are four main types of CSP systems:

- **Parabolic Troughs:** These curved mirrors focus sunlight onto a receiver tube running through the focal line. The fluid inside the tube is heated and used to generate steam for electricity.
- **Solar Towers:** Mirrors called heliostats are positioned around a central tower and track the sun's movement to focus sunlight onto a receiver at the top of the tower. The concentrated heat is then used to generate power.
- **Linear Fresnel Reflectors:** These systems use long rows of flat mirrors to focus sunlight onto a fixed receiver positioned above the mirrors.
- **Dish Stirling Systems:** These use a parabolic dish to focus sunlight onto a single point, where a Stirling engine converts the heat into mechanical energy, which is then used to generate electricity.

The biggest advantage of CSP over traditional solar panels is its ability to store energy in the form of heat, using **thermal energy storage** systems. For example, molten salt can retain heat for several hours, allowing CSP plants to generate electricity even after the sun goes down.

Key Advantages of CSP:

- Energy storage capability for night-time power generation.
- High efficiency in areas with strong direct sunlight.
- Scalability for large power plants.

Real-World Example:
The **Ivanpah Solar Power Facility** in California is one of the world's largest CSP plants, capable of producing 392 megawatts of power, enough to power 140,000 homes.

Chapter 3
Solar Water Heating and Thermal Energy

Solar water heating is one of the oldest and simplest uses of solar energy, and recent innovations have enhanced its efficiency and adaptability. Solar water heaters use solar collectors to absorb sunlight and transfer that heat to water. Solar heating systems can be applied for domestic water heating, space heating, or even industrial processes that require hot water.

There are two primary types of solar water heating systems:

- **Active Systems:** These systems use pumps to circulate water or heat-transfer fluids through the collectors and into a storage tank. Active systems are more efficient and can be used in colder climates where freezing might be an issue.
- **Passive Systems:** These systems rely on natural convection to move water through the collectors. Although they are less efficient than active systems, passive systems are cheaper and simpler to install, making them an attractive option for residential use.

Solar Thermal Energy for Industrial Applications:
Beyond domestic use, solar thermal energy can be harnessed for industrial purposes, including food processing, chemical manufacturing, and desalination. Solar thermal systems for industrial use often incorporate **concentrated solar thermal (CST)** technology, which can generate high temperatures needed for industrial processes.

Benefits of Solar Water Heating:

- Reduces the reliance on traditional heating fuels like gas or electricity.
- Lowers energy costs for homes and businesses.
- Provides a sustainable and renewable energy solution for both residential and industrial applications.

Chapter 4

Solar Windows and Building-Integrated Photovoltaics (BIPV)

Building-Integrated Photovoltaics (BIPV) represents a revolutionary shift in how solar energy is harnessed in urban environments. Instead of mounting traditional solar panels on rooftops, BIPV integrates solar cells directly into building materials such as windows, facades, and roofs. This allows for seamless energy generation without disrupting the aesthetic of the building.

One of the most promising developments in BIPV technology is **solar windows**. Solar windows use transparent or semi-transparent photovoltaic materials to capture sunlight while still allowing light to pass through. This innovation could turn every skyscraper into a solar power plant, significantly boosting the capacity for urban solar power generation.

Advantages of BIPV:

- Efficient use of space, especially in urban areas where roof space is limited.
- Aesthetically pleasing and easily integrated into building designs.
- Reduces energy consumption by generating electricity on-site.

Examples of BIPV Projects:

- **Tesla Solar Roof:** Roof tiles that act as solar panels but look like ordinary roof tiles.
- **Onyx Solar Windows:** Solar windows installed in buildings like the **PepsiCo headquarters** in New York.

Chapter 5
Solar Paint and Coatings

Solar paint is a cutting-edge innovation that could revolutionize the solar energy market by making it easier to integrate solar power into a wider range of surfaces. Instead of installing bulky panels, solar paint consists of a liquid solution embedded with photovoltaic nanoparticles. These nanoparticles capture sunlight and convert it into electricity, much like traditional solar cells.

Solar paint could be applied to walls, roofs, vehicles, or even clothing, turning everyday surfaces into energy-generating devices. Although still in the experimental stages, solar paint shows great promise for the future of solar energy.

How Solar Paint Works:

- **Photovoltaic nanoparticles** in the paint absorb sunlight and generate electricity.
- The paint can be applied like any other coating, making it versatile and easy to deploy.

Applications of Solar Paint:

- Buildings: Turning entire buildings into power generators.
- Vehicles: Reducing reliance on traditional fuel by generating solar energy on the go.
- Consumer Products: Clothing or backpacks that generate power for personal devices.

Chapter 6
Solar Energy in Space

Space-based solar power (SBSP) is an ambitious concept that involves collecting solar energy in space and transmitting it back to Earth via microwave or laser beams. Solar panels placed in orbit could capture sunlight 24/7, without the interference of Earth's atmosphere or weather patterns, making SBSP a continuous source of clean energy.

Advantages of Space-Based Solar Power:

- Constant sunlight without atmospheric interference.
- Potential to generate much more energy than ground-based solar systems.
- Can be transmitted to any location on Earth, even remote areas.

While still in its early stages, space agencies like NASA and private companies are investigating the feasibility of SBSP as a large-scale solution to the global energy crisis.

Chapter 7

Solar-Powered Transportation

The use of solar energy in transportation is an exciting and rapidly growing field. Solar-powered vehicles offer the promise of zero-emission travel powered entirely by renewable energy. Several prototypes and operational vehicles already demonstrate the potential of solar-powered transportation.

Innovations in Solar Transportation:

- **Solar Cars:** Vehicles like the **Lightyear One** use solar panels embedded in the roof to extend their driving range, harnessing the sun's energy directly.
- **Solar Planes:** The **Solar Impulse 2** aircraft completed a flight around the world using only solar energy, demonstrating the viability of solar-powered aviation.
- **Solar Boats:** Solar-powered yachts and ferries are being developed for use in the maritime industry, offering a cleaner alternative to traditional fuel.

Solar Highways and Roads:
In addition to solar vehicles, innovations such as **solar highways** are being tested. Solar roads are built with solar panels embedded in the surface, capable of generating electricity while supporting traffic. These roads could power streetlights, electric vehicles, and even nearby buildings.

Chapter 8
Agrivoltaics: Solar Energy and Agriculture

Agrivoltaics is a practice that combines solar energy production with agriculture, optimizing the use of land by generating electricity and growing crops on the same land. Solar panels can provide shade to crops, reducing water evaporation and protecting them from extreme heat while also producing electricity.

Benefits of Agrivoltaics:

- Improves the efficiency of land use by combining two productive activities.
- Protects crops from climate extremes and reduces water needs.
- Generates additional income for farmers by selling surplus energy.

Case Study:
In **Japan**, agrivoltaics is used to grow crops like lettuce and herbs under solar panels while generating enough electricity to power local homes and businesses.

Chapter 9

Solar Energy Storage Innovations

One of the biggest challenges with solar energy is its intermittent nature—the sun doesn't shine at night or during cloudy days. **Energy storage** technologies are critical for addressing this limitation, allowing solar energy to be stored and used when sunlight is not available.

Innovations in Solar Storage:

- **Flow Batteries:** These large-scale batteries use liquid electrolytes to store solar energy efficiently over long periods.
- **Molten Salt Storage:** Used in CSP systems, molten salt can store solar heat for several hours, allowing power generation even after sunset.
- **Solid-State Batteries:** These batteries offer higher energy density and longer lifespans than traditional lithium-ion batteries, making them ideal for solar energy storage.

By improving energy storage solutions, we can overcome one of the major barriers to the widespread adoption of solar energy and create a more reliable, 24/7 clean energy supply.

Chapter 10
The Future of Solar Energy: What's Next?

The future of solar energy is full of exciting possibilities. New technologies and innovations are continually pushing the boundaries of what solar energy can achieve. By combining solar energy with other renewable energy sources like wind and geothermal, we can create **hybrid systems** that are more reliable and efficient.

Emerging Trends:

- **Artificial Intelligence in Solar:** AI and machine learning algorithms are being used to optimize the performance of solar power plants and maximize efficiency.

- **Decentralized Solar Networks:** Peer-to-peer energy trading allows individuals and communities to generate and trade solar energy directly, reducing reliance on centralized utilities.

- **Floating Solar Farms:** Solar panels can be placed on bodies of water, such as reservoirs and lakes, to generate electricity without taking up land space.

As technology continues to evolve, solar energy will play an even larger role in meeting the world's energy needs, helping to mitigate climate change and create a more sustainable future.

Glossary - Solar Energy Innovations: Beyond Solar Panels:

1. **Active Solar Heating** – A system that uses mechanical or electrical equipment, such as pumps or fans, to actively collect, store, and distribute solar energy for heating purposes.

2. **Alternating Current (AC)** – The type of electrical current used in most homes and businesses, which is converted from the direct current (DC) produced by solar panels.

3. **Balance of System (BOS)** – The components of a solar energy system aside from the photovoltaic panels, including wiring, inverters, and mounting hardware.

4. **Batteries** – Energy storage devices that store excess solar power for later use, especially important in off-grid or hybrid systems.

5. **Battery Management System (BMS)** – A system that monitors and regulates the charging and discharging of a battery to ensure safety and efficiency.

6. **BIPV (Building-Integrated Photovoltaics)** – Solar technologies that are integrated into the building materials, such as windows or roofs, rather than mounted on top of them.

7. **Capacity Factor** – The ratio of the actual energy output of a solar power plant compared to its maximum possible output over a given period.

8. **Carbon Footprint** – The total greenhouse gas emissions caused directly or indirectly by an individual, organization, event, or product, which solar energy helps reduce.

9. **Clean Energy** – Energy derived from renewable, non-polluting sources such as solar, wind, and hydropower.

10. **Concentrated Solar Power (CSP)** – A system that uses mirrors or lenses to concentrate sunlight onto a small area to generate heat, which is then used to produce electricity.

11. **Curtailment** – The reduction of energy output from renewable sources, including solar, due to lack of demand or grid constraints.

12. **DC (Direct Current)** – The type of electrical current produced by solar panels, which must be converted to alternating current (AC) by an inverter for most uses.

13. **Decentralized Energy Systems** – Localized energy systems that

generate and consume energy close to the source, reducing reliance on centralized power grids.

14. **Distributed Generation (DG)** – Small-scale power generation technologies (like solar PV systems) that are located close to the point of consumption.

15. **Dual-Axis Tracker** – A tracking system that moves solar panels in two directions (up/down and left/right) to follow the sun's movement and increase energy capture.

16. **Energy Conversion Efficiency** – The percentage of sunlight that a solar panel converts into usable electrical energy.

17. **Feed-in Tariff (FiT)** – A policy mechanism that encourages renewable energy production by offering long-term contracts to producers for the electricity they generate.

18. **Floating Solar** – Solar power systems that are installed on bodies of water, such as lakes or reservoirs, to save land space and increase efficiency.

19. **Grid Parity** – The point at which the cost of solar-generated electricity is equal to or less than the cost of electricity from the grid.

20. **Grid-Tied System** – A solar energy system that is connected to the public electricity grid, allowing users to sell excess energy back to the grid.

21. **Heliostat** – A device equipped with mirrors that follow the movement of the sun and concentrate sunlight onto a central point for energy generation.

22. **Hybrid Solar System** – A solar energy system that combines solar power with other energy sources (such as wind or diesel generators) or with battery storage.

23. **Insolation** – The amount of solar radiation reaching a given area, typically measured in kilowatt-hours per square meter per day (kWh/m^2/day).

24. **Inverter** – A device that converts direct current (DC) electricity from solar panels into alternating current (AC) electricity for use in homes or businesses.

25. **Kilowatt (kW)** – A unit of power equal to 1,000 watts, used to measure the output capacity of solar panels.

26. **Kilowatt-Hour (kWh)** – A unit of energy representing the amount of electricity consumed or generated, equivalent to using one kilowatt of power for one hour.

27. **Levelized Cost of Energy (LCOE)** – A measure of the average cost per unit of electricity generated over the lifetime of a solar energy system.

28. **Microgrid** – A localized energy grid that can operate independently from the main electrical grid, often incorporating renewable energy sources like solar power.

29. **Monocrystalline Solar Cells** – A type of photovoltaic cell made from a single, continuous crystal structure, known for higher efficiency compared to polycrystalline cells.

30. **MPPT (Maximum Power Point Tracking)** – A technology used in solar inverters to optimize the power output from solar panels by adjusting electrical loads.

31. **Net Metering** – A billing arrangement that credits solar energy system owners for the excess electricity they generate and send back to the grid.

32. **Off-grid System** – A solar energy system that operates independently from the main electrical grid, typically relying on battery storage for continuous power.

33. **Overproduction** – When a solar system generates more electricity than is needed at a particular time, often sending excess power back to the grid.

34. **Passive Solar Design** – Building designs that use the sun's natural energy for heating, cooling, and lighting, without the use of mechanical devices.

35. **Photovoltaic (PV)** – Technology that converts sunlight directly into electricity using semiconductor materials, commonly found in solar panels.

36. **Polycrystalline Solar Cells** – Solar cells made from multiple silicon crystals, offering a lower-cost alternative to monocrystalline cells but generally with lower efficiency.

37. **Power Purchase Agreement (PPA)** – A contract between a solar energy provider and a consumer where the provider sells electricity generated from a solar system at a fixed rate.

38. **Renewable Energy Credits (RECs)** – Certificates representing the environmental benefits of generating electricity from renewable energy sources, which can be sold or traded.

39. **Reverse Auction** – A method used by governments or utilities to procure solar energy by allowing developers to bid to supply electricity at the lowest possible price.

40. **Solar Cell** – The basic unit of a solar panel that converts sunlight into electrical energy.

41. **Solar Collector** – A device that captures and absorbs solar radiation, converting it into heat or electricity.

42. **Solar Farm** – A large-scale solar installation composed of many solar panels that generate electricity for commercial or utility-scale use.

43. **Solar Inverter** – A device that converts the direct current (DC) electricity generated by solar panels into alternating current (AC) for use in the electrical grid or home.

44. **Solar Radiation** – The electromagnetic radiation, including visible light, emitted by the sun that can be harnessed to generate electricity or heat.

45. **Solar Shingles** – Roof tiles that function as photovoltaic panels, providing both a building's structural covering and a source of solar power.

46. **Solar Thermal** – Technology that uses the sun's heat to produce energy, often for heating water or generating electricity in solar thermal power plants.

47. **Thin-Film Solar Cells** – Solar cells made by layering thin sheets of photovoltaic material onto a substrate, known for flexibility and lightweight applications.

48. **Tracking System** – A system that adjusts the orientation of solar panels or mirrors to follow the sun throughout the day, increasing energy capture.

49. **Virtual Power Plant (VPP)** – A network of decentralized energy sources, such as solar panels and battery storage, managed collectively to provide energy like a traditional power plant.

50. **Zero-Energy Building (ZEB)** – A building that produces as much energy as it consumes over the course of a year, often through a combination of solar power and energy-efficient design.

www.ingramcontent.com/pod-product-compliance
Lightning Source LLC
Chambersburg PA
CBHW030042230526
45472CB00002B/632